Weathers Permitting

GAYLORD			PRINTED IN U.S.A.

VN
IES

POETRY BY STEPHEN SANDY

Weathers Permitting

Stephen Sandy POEMS

LOUISIANA STATE UNIVERSITY PRESS

BATON ROUGE

Designer: Andrew Shurtz
Typeface: Quadraat
Printer and binder: Thomson-Shore, Inc.

Library of Congress Cataloging-in-Publication Data

Sandy, Stephen.
    Weathers permitting : poems / Stephen Sandy.
        p. cm.
    ISBN 0-8071-3001-x (hardcover : alk. paper) —
    ISBN 0-8071-3002-8 (pbk. : alk. paper)
    I. Title.
PS3569.A52W43 2005
811'.54—dc22

                                    2004021596

The paper in this book meets the guidelines for permanence
and durability of the Committee on Production Guidelines
for Book Longevity of the Council on Library Resources.
∞

for Julia Randall

Contents

Weathers Permitting

Instructions for Planting a Pine Woodlot

In early September,
      gather the cones.
When dry air in a spare
      room opens them,
beat out the seed; at once, sow; and shelter
      three years. Your seedlings then
are planted (if boxboard is all you want)
      ten feet apart.

If clear timber—the best
      quality—four
feet each way so that they
      grow tall and straight,
losing their lower limbs. Too densely sown,
      in tangles the sprouts fail—
mere straw; too far, and branches knot the trunks.
      A near presence,

near exactly enough
      without being
too near, induces a
      concentrated
vertical thrust. Fifteen years the trees grow
      four feet apart. At this
point, thin out half; screened from light by linked twigs,
      the shoots perish.

High as you can reach, prune
      branches. Thirty
years, and your trees will be
      mature—firm now,
and on course. You can't stop thinning, though, for
      thirty more—or the best
trunks get caught at crown height, or in root jams
      in their deep soils.

At last (though this may be
　　long after your
concern has fallen off)
　　each surviving
trunk will have attained to a size which lets
　　it stand, affected by
no other life the black earth can put forth.
　　Setting a slow,

steady pace (still at it
　　whole centuries
later), no thing can harm
　　them as they rise
onward, nothing—but blows of sleet or wind
　　or fire, or the long
appraising eye of the inheritor
　　of your woodlot.

One

Stillness

Blue bearded iris so tall it bloomed
in the lower apple branches. Ice
tinkling in tea was like the sound
of ankles' muted clicking when
she did her set-up exercise
on the floor. Later by the lake
where ordinary people not in love
walked up and down he heard the ice

crackle in a glass of white. That creak
was like the snap her bra straps made
on shoulders when she slipped them on.
The Chablis waited while she gave
the boy his lesson in the leafy shade,
pergola where honeysuckle trails.

Cardinals

What now: the cardinal in the maple
fills the air for all in earshot;
its monody, nonsense streaming
    down to my ear.

What then: in the plumb of noon I heard
a call somewhere from blowsy elms;
she answered with mimetic trills.
    So it responded,

a dialogue, played phrasings back
and back. I hear the song now, but not
her whistling or the wind on the lake,
    whitecaps below.

Now any cardinal recalls her,
repeats its melody—O not
for her as when she called; yet clear
    for me, noting

a bird's call or the lucid boom
of jet, or snarl a stranger's power
mower belts to a neighborhood,
    to a ringing ear.

Rain Date

His daughter had gone off again to church.
He sat with tea, papaya, and day-old chips
watching the rain, not feeling left in the lurch
by this—but puzzled at the odd ellipse:
surely she wasn't enamoured of the pale
Galilean on the shore—apocalypse
yet further from her mind. She might avail
herself of fellow feelings that would eclipse
the dailiness of things. It was their company
she warmed to. He, seduced by a helter-skelter
of distractions, imported teachings duty-free—
and by these guesses only now half guessed—
turned from the rituals that once gave shelter,
from principal returned without the interest.

Stable

The ornaments they made at home from dough,
taut origami stars and paper snowflakes
scissored fresh each year, argued some lack
beside those gauds decking designer trees
such as the absent neighbor's window framed.
That year the boozy Santa carved in the Black
Forest and the dainty reindeer of Venetian glass—
their flanks aglow with distorting mirrors—gave way

to a 1957 Chevrolet
in aqua resin and an early combat jet,
replicas weighing branchlets down, floating from gold
tethers. Now they had licenses, they drove
to shopping malls; the trove of pleasures swelled
to a remembered mass. That year the children
abandoned the mossy crèche in its pasteboard box;
only some cattle and a Bengal tiger took the air

—toy horde that kids crosslegged on a sweatshop floor
all day in India whittled then lacquered there—
ranged in procession on a table, heading
to no stable. In the dark above their eaves
a train of Canada geese, one year unable
to finish their journey by the solstice, called
to each other in the clouds, circled for bearings,
wheeling and wheeling above the lamplit street.

Home Reel

The projector jumps, the foxes around her neck,
not rabid, are holding on, each biting, glass-eyed,
the other's tail. She clambers to the running board
of the Franklin, smiles at us, steps to the house to make
a start. Cut to the fence, the hollyhocks,
and Roddy the red setter nipping sips
from the sprinkler spurting; harnessed, pulling Mopsie
in the red wagon, wagging for master, who looks
then catches all of them lolling below the smoke.
In Florida once, he filmed a shambling bear
who danced—who jigs for us still in his grim gear.

Stop by the fencing, child, and slowly meet them,
a world within the world, a garden walk
to take with them to the portiere, the parlor, scent
of humidor unlidded. They pose on the steps
doffing golf caps; none may read their moving lips.

Bottleshard

Delving a half foot down
where the lane by Hiland Farm
ran once—or no, this must
have been the midden, close
as an arm's easy toss
from a calico-curtained window
of the farmhouse kitchen—now
she dug a bed to put in
scallions, lettuce, basil,
parsley, sage. She knelt.
Her finger rubbed the soil
from a relic shard, now silken;
she eyed it shining back
bright with a fleck of sky,
sharp flash of broken glass.

She held the octagon,
extracted bit of green
bottle, letters embossed
on its side, *O W*, as if to
warn her of its blade points.
She held it to the light
this way and that; now
it read *M O* as if
there were more of it to come;
but she probed with trowel and found
no more; turning it over
she read out *W O*
as if to mark some end,
then *O M* as if to set her
down, grounded in prayer.

Behind their house on the hill
above the lake, her father
put up a pylon once,

two-by-sixes to hang
a swing from, gravel oblong
beneath it edged with planks;
then a trestle, lower,
so the boys could reach it,
grip at the iron bar,
and hang there swinging, waiting
for biceps strong enough
to do a chin-up, hanging,
aching to please, to mind
a boy's duty, code of
machismo already stirring

in edgy striplings. Yes,
days turned from Fragonard-dimpled
children swinging under
the high umbrella dome
of elm shade to the work
of growing a body. Those
chin-ups soon would make it
strong; *no swinging now,*
hold the body limp
except for arms and hold
on tight, that-a-way now,
pull. Soon manly arms
from a boy's stringy body,
and she would watch them, swinging,
not told to do those things.

Until the day she looked,
she had not feared the earth,
the ghost-hung dark, the tiger
under the bed. She peeked
over the edge of the gravel
trough that caved inward,
a sudden funneling down,
descent that Father had lit
a torch to show, and dropped

the gas-soaked rag—a shirt once—
down. Down it flickered, forever
burning smaller, twisting;
she peered until it winkled
out in nightmare darkness
and silence. The back yard was

off-limits then, forbidden
until two four-ton trucks
and backhoe filled it up,
load after load of fill,
gray gargantuan pailfuls.
At last the glacial till
topped out at playground level
by the chinning bar, cesspool
cavern an emptiness filled,
fossil funnel; air
no more. She watched for days
until a load of lake sand
made a sandbox, or something
like a sandbox. She thought
she would not swing there, over

that ground—so what if dump trucks
filled it in as might be?—
in there somewhere the little
ragged sleeve of gaslit
shirt was burning. Instead,
she wandered downhill, down
where a brickwalled well, a wide
manhole someone had lifted
the lid aside from, lay open,
gaping. Rungs descended;
she climbed—or did she fall?—
down there; sat at the bottom
by a gauge or pipe valve there,
musing with the Raggedy
Ann she carried, looking

at the circle shard of sky,
wondering what was up.
Betimes, her mother sent
the boys to find their sister.
Traipsing downhill, one saw
two circles on the grass, peeked
at the darker lip to find
her peering up. Rung
by rung he clambered down
to help (she might have climbed
herself, but fright had kept her).
Years later she was digging now
with care, still wondering what
was down there, within; what
it was she hoped to find.

Long Lake

Dark movings loading unloading
against the dawn the busied captain
gearing up; the boy of two
minds two feelings rather—cold
watches of misty distance where
invisible loons from their dark would send
annunciating cries. As if
in flight across the lake the ten-horse
outboard fled the roar severing
calms slapping the keel down loud
on black then silvered waters the boy
like a figurehead guiding, guarding,
parted the wind, the grip of it, brow
at the thudding prow the engine driving
to light seeping from eastern cloudwall
to communion or silence, at least the father
astern steering and child forward
bellow of speed balancing stillness
till favored bay was found—how
did he know where it was in those
indifferent glassy runes, flatlands
lapping their sides? Then two hours
business only the tackle the baiting
of hooks then reeling in. With a catch
they would turn about now, black sheet
ripped by the outboard's whipcord yelp
spouting delirious fumes, exhaust
merging with bilge oil, catch aboard
on a line tied to the gunwhale, fish smell—
rainbow of, for him, *at last.*

Easiness trading off for talk,
speech canceled racing the backstretch,
they homed to food and inside soon
or escape at least from piscatorial

rite, this bridge the father made,
he whom the boy had made his mind up
to make into another body,
stranger he knew the back of. He scanned
the shoreline watched it enlarge, divulge
assuring outlines cottonwood now
then path cutting high grass to rental
cabin, brightening hour promising
news, the day already fusing
with pine smell, fire on windowpane—
there, gleaming relic of sunrise.

Safe Mode

Safety was sitting tight until they found
whatever was on the fritz, what fuse went dead,
and it got fixed—he did as the others did.
In the Navy things went snafu as when the squad

marched to the VD film. The geared reel strained,
film jumped; on screen the obscene dick
pulsed, when the kid behind him shuddered, leaned
forward, and shot breakfast across his neck.

Squad mates snickered, the marine in charge growled
from darkness *knock it off*. The sailor cried
in awful pain, but now the laughter had spread
with the odor . . . camera panned up urinal,

paused at a steel bar the voice-over said
was there for men with doses to grip, as needed.
The bar was bent from shape by straining hands.
—Cut to the suited floosie, high shoulders padded,

and soon to her den, her bamboo blinds and chintz
bedspread. The tipsy gob tumbles, embracing her.
The guy's not heard of the clap—*well maybe, just once* . . .
Meanwhile the magma is trekking down his jumper

and he is a seaman recruit without defect—
so far—head down, not once put *on report*.
How much better to stay put, he fancies; abort
to safe mode, maybe winning the squad's respect.

Castlerigg

We followed in Keats's footsteps to the Stone
Circle, his "Druid Temple"; found its cold
jaws agape, each stone ground to a knurl
as if from chewing the cud of sun and storm
for eons. You traipsed to the car in a Tokyo sulk,
sat grim till I, amazed, returned.
                              Your grudging
college colleagues, when leftist youngsters swarmed
their Todai halls, in the heat of noon once hurled
insults up at their students—their young; called,
"You're African savages!" These urban men
enjoy their learning, status, coats of silk;
shun origins as if forbidden knowledge.

Occasional

They said the day it fell it was just at noon.
Scattered bells tolled over the quarter. He walked
in crowds shopping. Dusty construction workers
nimble in jodhpurs climbed down from curtained scaffolds
for lunch. He made his way to a noodle shop
where, just as he ordered, the screen began to show
a kind of temple gate, a sort of ramada:
suspended from it a bell, an immense barrel.
Customers paused in their chatting and eating and started
to look up, to listen—the clapper, a great beam,
swung in and boomed against the rim of bronze.
Everyone froze remembering, turned from the screen
and looked. He stared down into the deep bowl
of ramen before him. Then it was over—glances
turned to old manners when he rose from his stool,
then out into streets steaming like a bathhouse,
smog green as algae, sweet with taxi fumes.
A woman wrapped in her indigo cotton paused
near him, smiling, bowing. Men oblivious
in their dark Western suits, smoking, marching
to offices; talking, passing the hours, intent
on a long workday ending and drinks together.
The crowd closed ranks around him. It moved along.

Hamster Hotel

Hamster Abuse on Benmont Avenue
—*newspaper headline*

A man watches
everyone caring

about the rodent—
arrests and public

exposure—across
the page from people

bodies like whey
washed up on red

Rwanda banks
so far so red so dark,

the man is a lover
and cannot

turn the page.

Ghazal for Geldzahler

I met this modest fellow in the dorm; it was kind Henry.
Among the tall suits and lofty shirts, no one could find Henry

but it wouldn't be long before he got ahead. Soon few were left
to say, just look at him, or, pay no mind to Henry.

The years were kind. I got a letter from the Metropolitan:
who could it be? It was a laughing note—signed, Henry.

Later he wore hats of many colors and sat to everyone
(go figure, Andy!) who wanted to spellbind Henry

and let him give a hand. And Henry, willing, clambered among
his buddies up; O bully fellow with big cigar, Henry!

Now nothing would do among his modern chairs and elder griefs;
he was a king but sad with his cigar, dear Henry.

O dratted times! A most even hum: a curse, and even
a blessing for us still at it, close or far, behind Henry.

On Looking into Lattimore's Homer

I knew these men who died, and all gone down
in the velocity of a month
about the time it took Achilles
to get over his sulk about the girl
and out onto the field of Ilium again. Tony
whose heart jumped him just as his train
pulled into Penn Station
down there in the dark underworld coursing along
in tunnels beside the subways
darkness roaring and the snapshooting
windows of passing cars passengers
nursing their wounds crowds
standing by on platforms
thinking about glory the glory they never quite won
to go along with the supper they did

or Jack who didn't want anyone to know
he was dying because he needed that shame
all for himself needed to complete
his life alone that beautiful life he planned
back in the tenements of Philadelphia sixty years
back when he heard a Brahms quintet
flow from a window and knew if he practiced enough
diligence would make his shield and his bow
and he would shine with the resin of a divine protection

or Don whom I remember fresh from having
his last tooth pulled searching the dump each Saturday
for useful gear something of value things
to furnish his ratty cape with stuff that might
come in handy unable to live with dishonor
the letter from H—— years before that read, "I conclude
that graduate study is not your dish of tea"

and Jim who was given much who knew
what fortune meant retainer of a lord
he returned what he'd been given tenfold
kept going onward up ahead
once again I look for you
after the performance as we'd agreed before it
once more I cannot find you
evidence quickly mounts that you
have gone down among the others.
Have a good season then and may you find shelter, all,
from heat; cool baths, unstinted portions
of roasted meats and wines for feasting.

Two

Iris

The toad in his
    socket of mud
like a lump of
    tiger's-eye pudding

clambering stumbling
    toward hosta shade,
tumbling back
    into time—he

was barely breathing
    I thought when I
touched him. Or was he
    exhaling only

like the wet loam
    and the rhizomes
gyring into green
    spears, fistful

of swagger sticks
    under the sun's arm?

Natural History: A Barn

When I came to this hill the sun
at noon the men were pinning
poker hands on a sapling warm
words a remembrance for Chuck
who had died—the full
houses and pairs a straight flush
fluttered called on an afternoon and
someone tied one an ace to label
the trunk and the smiles drank a toast

now the maple has a hundred arms
reaching up from the place once
a barnyard straight for the sky ten thousand
leaves flash in a sulphurous globe
simmer gold in wind off the mountain
I am not sure what protected that
straight growing but the walls
for years I walked down the aisle
where stanchions hung once

out through wide cow door spaces
the wing where hogs had lived sows
in their pens litters frisking in straw
by open windows gone
the separator room near the silo
half toilet half work station now
a pin oak leaf on the casement sill
umber witness going and entering
it has the place in heedless freehold

the fall its own imperative this way
one morning cattle led downhill to
auction when the yard became ours
a courtyard with grass and years
since I could hold the trunk

in my fist as if I were shaking
a man's hand now it takes
two arms to hold as if I
hold someone's waist in a dance

too near to shake the hand of
like a friend and it is only a tree
intent on what it is doing there
rooted where I have walked when
the wind blew with snow not leaves
what has happened
I wonder and look for food
for the bun I left on a saucer
on my shelf next to the Milton

not even a crumb it is gone
vanished—
tiny swart cylinders litter
poxing the shelves droppings
like caraway seeds thrown
from across the room the shelf
and the saucer evenly spread as if
with care but here are three
on the next shelf near the Williams:

Blake and Wordsworth food is
gone wrought in the guts of the living
mice who came in the night
intending no harm eating my
lunch. There is an emergency
generator these days beyond
the window in the field strewn with
dark legumes of the honey locust
writhing to rattles fallen into

November from this distance
black pods like mouse pats but
I am hearing the wringing grind

of the generator that snarls
harsh whirring through which
men women boys must walk
waiting to get through the sound
barrier before they are free
to use speech again

they huddle and hasten as if
caught in a wind peppery
with frost with the blue hills
turning to ice the wind plummets
off the end of the world I
cannot hear their words they
could not hear mine those words
might be coming across but only
a generator gets them—folds them

away launders them in its jarring
roar to a sparkling momentary
stillness. Deep in dry honeysuckle
years by the busiest door
a slight nest shows up when
leaves go it is beaten down
by rains now shallow as if
it had winced to know the weather
pitiful saucer holding now

only a few curled tiny leaves
who knows what bird a small bird
odd place for a bird Phil says. One
of the minor singers a sparrow perhaps.
Only spot of nature in the courtyard
it could find but now December
and no sparrows sing or clamor
in the eaves it seems now
for one of our friendly songbirds

an unfit place somehow the best
it could do there is a chance
it knew it had the courtyard
to itself a slight burgundy tint
edged with scarlet on a few
twigs that glow in the low
warm of December sun
like berries on a wreath
on a crown aflame midnights.

In the barn the rats clamber
up on the drink machine
they peer into the trash bin
if anything looks good
they go for it—
tails and claws against
Styrofoam squeal of
covered lunch trays where some
sandwich someone was too full

to finish got heaped a grease-
smell tuna melt all over
by the drink machine corner—
when one finishes he doesn't
go back up on the machine
he climbs down and maunders
along the empty hall past the exit
light shedding its ruddy glow
over the uneven blind-nailed floor.

Provider

In shade of the walnut trees
at the end of the garden he digs
to plant seedlings, keeps
at it through curtains of heat.
He need not hurry, or so

he thought, but then he knew.
The mosquitoes the midges
the greenheads don't see he's there
until the sweat begins,
maybe with smell of soap

or worn work boots. A thimble
of trace odors but
enough for fine olfactory
radars. Soon they lock on,
out for blood—descending

on every limb. Spade work
is done—he trundles a wheel
barrow to ready trays
pursued by his insects. They,
like his seedlings, rely on him.

Sonam Lama

He and his helper sang together
while they set each quarried slab in place
until a wall of Goshen stone
shored up the slope by the apple trees.

Sonam Lama stands in morning sun,
hands on hips, surveying his wall,
thinking of—what? Some matter
no doubt of home, which was in Lhasa,
above the high passes.

We praise the fitted stones
that lie sanely by each other
holding each other in place.

Days later, leaf mold soil fills in
behind the wall. Already
from the apple, windfalls tumble
across his work, cluster;
mandala on the loam; fresh earth.

Opera Orchard

Let me wander there
great terra-cotta conchs
    cradled from boughs

browned with sandalwood
incense, tinder, charcoal
    briquettes, brief cloudlets

ascending to Major Jennings'
heaven, September sky.
Call the majors of Handel's

joyful ear, while flute
leads on Rebecca, her
    bold vibrato,

and tree frogs, soon awakened
through every apple tree,
    take up the strain.

Reliquary

Nothing enhances its beauty
hand-swelled shape
like the kill hole
in the base of a Hopi bowl
by which it may
escape the orbit of

utility—it lets air
through then dedicates
this vessel to
the spirit which called it
out from sunflecked
low-fired banks of delta

river that daily
caves some of itself
in on the slick
mud of tidal flat
faltering in runoffs fresh
waters moiling with salt.

Three

Worn Tool

How odd to hold this implement
        of a lapsed time

whose dated use clings still in the
        blunt blade and the

gleaming grip—Celtic chimera,
        brave lion head

softened by hands. Soon even you
        will be forgotten,

my letter opener, bronze or brass!
        No one will know

why such a dull stub of a blade
        found such a fanciful

handle, as if the one who gripped it
        fought with ghosts.

Conclusion

Icarus: his two white legs
sticking out of the
sea, making a victory sign.

Prepared Piano

Spotting a shell that gleams there, you wonder, why go for it,
this one, among them all on the beach? I go for it.

A walk, any walk, every walk has a daub that gleams back,
but you may miss it, looking too low or high: go for it

anyway. A manatee is a rock in a matinee world,
which is not Yeats's gossamer world, not Sligo, for it

will knee your crotch if you stick up your nose at it. Go
crack the monkey's skull for a dish; dig in. Oh my, go for it

if you want to look cool. Pick up your chopsticks, tong out
some brains, smack your lips, eat it and sigh. Go for it

while you're still conscious, don't faint on me now!
Or go back where gulls circle, hover, and slow, for it

's your sandy tideline where birds, evil—or almost evil—
spot a lone creature, beached but moving; hover, and go for it.

Rain Crow

He shakes himself awake; reconnoiters; caws
to Tom or Dick or Jerry, of this fox he saw.
Taunting his groundlings, manic for applause.

Then off he sails trailing crow calls, rau-
cous as gale-whipped branches cracking; saurian, raw
brassy cries, hungrier than any appetite
he ever had. Long hollow wing bones, maw
packed with marrow, lock in position—bright
feathers slick with light. Is it to complain
he rides the updraft, tacking?
                    Cruising elohim
in a black coat, wings hovering like temple eaves,
gives shelter, now here now there, from the rain,
moving across parcels of earth below him;
the barren plots, the fields bound up in sheaves.

Drier Air

Are you making things up as you go along?
What's happening, calling me by your name?

Limpid eyes blacken. Wade for oblivion.
Have I abandoned you, Mother, to stones?

White-face hornets live in the garden dirt, change
the shape of my arm when I pick a flower.

These days I'm the definition of *edgy*.
But I was at home in my body once, too.

ACs whir all over town, yet the bright cleome
need only a pinch of roots like hairs from a sage's chin.

O shift in basic paradigm! No one will read this.
No one will hear the last tango in Auschwitz.

Limpid eyes blacken. Wade for oblivion.
Have I abandoned you, Mother, to stones?

Above Como

Granite risers, zigzag cobble stairs,
crazy-quilt flagstone, riprap; cementblock booths

sheltering Stations of the Cross, glazed figure
bending low; another, there, reaching;

tile small as bathroom tile at home; red, blue
and gold show from a gloom of soiled guard screens.

Climb and climb; query moss-clad stones;
at every turn, mute rockface; goat-pocked cliffside,

goatfold below: why climb toward empty space,
the heart drumming, tolling under his shirt?

*

With friends he went to make the climb,
switchbacked ascent to a stone facade
on a cliff, high up a mountain's flank,
so high you only saw it when sunset
picked out its rampart briefly, unlikely
edifice at such an altitude.

Theirs was no pilgrimage, only a jaunt
to explore, but like true mountaineers
they'd do it since . . . since there it was
to do. They walked the cobbled alleys
quaintly leading out of town
to pastures, trails above tiled roofs. . . .

Later, they found they could not do
some things they lacked the know-how to.
They paused at first one Station then

another, but pressed onward, upward.
Soon, one grew short of breath, fell back.
The laggard heard his heart and thought,

forget the higher ridge—there's one,
with a chapel all its own, a stage
halfway, or less than halfway, up.
He saw, from the grassy bower trees made,
a plane, diminished by distance, drift
quavering far below. He turned,

watching them trudge above him there
emerging in sunlight from a cleft
like specks along the cliff wall's top—
Michael, Ellen, Todd, his friends
ever closer to the turret's outcrop
until they vanished, lost in distance.

★

At the memorial chapel
of *Gruppo Alpino Griante*
someone had raised a flag—
scarlet, white, and green.
There was time to reconnoiter

waiting for them, and loiter
hearing the world he left
yield its frail stir below.
Someone had put flowers
in the dented pewter urn

behind the padlocked grille.
Twenty-four—two plaques
gave every name—fell
in the First, fourteen
in the Second War, plus four

shipped to the Russian Front.
Their plaster eagle fiercely
climbed the wall, a cannon
gripped in its talons, Alps
white silhouettes below.

*

In Thessaly, they sang
how Herakles, triumphant
on a mountain headland, prayed
to be acknowledged by
the god he thought his father;

but vengeance felled him there,
shirt drenched in centaur blood.
On her lookout, the dying heiress
abandoning her book
above the weald of the world

would brood from her Alpine ledge
on kingdoms; on the wealth
she was; would turn, climb down.
So was the laggard fortunate
on a mountain chapel's plot

of grass, no terrace for
renunciation. How many
mornings had been, would be.
Then breath came slow and cool
until a gust of wind—

as sun drove under cloud—
bid him shiver. Finding
that vacant corner, intimate
precipice, he did,
not knowing how he did.

Ohio in Italy

Artful dodger, like the sumac
that grew regardless, tough
stuff that spread in the night, he
called *hell* to anybody
watching. It was like

that afternoon Wright saw
quattrocento, golden—
Jim with his luggage of
terrible need—met Giotto
in Padua, so moved by

that removed perfection of
mass then color then grace
he knew it was art, stark,
apocalyptic but
like Dante's sestina not

something that helped; alien,
ambered stuff, and far
from verbalizing with him
about that awful niche
between need and joy—far

from helping as the blood-red
sumac in Martins Ferry,
bird beshat invader,
wily and lovely squatter
that cried, *out of my way.*

Halloween Away

1

Slow afternoons close in; a mop
of sleet swipes at the window, blots
the view. Doing time in a distant town,

I watch two teams, the Boys and the Bills
butting each other, helmets and visors
    clamping heads, like Bosch's idea of Martians.

Far off, I see your puzzled smile
held onto in exhausted rage
    at a body slowly quitting: until the night

the twenty-thousand dollar machine
permitting breath abandoned you—
    or you abandoned it. Now, in this other

climate where I wait, the hollies
gleam, green in spite of frost,
    and berries like scarlet raindrops glaze, then freeze.

2

I reach to touch a branch; the branch—
barbed leaves twisted like a hand
    half closing to a fist—reaches back

and catches, ready to claw my hand
or anything to its dark shining.
    I break a sprig off, remembering the nude

immediate of your way, far from
hyperbole of muscle, of speed,
    and know as if for certain that you have died

a thousand miles away in the frozen
alba of Monday morning. Once
  you worked a laptop with some help and heard

your river, music, its own resource,
azure Itaska lapping lazy
  shores far in the North. There in twilight

your eyes would roll with pleasure when
I played your Beethoven CD.
  You wanted to know what was beyond—not any

old idea of death, but this
one gate hung in the wall of light
  in the sun ahead of you, something beyond

the drift of Szigeti's violin
or that old, irreplaceable
  recording of the Missa Solemnis. But common

wisdom held you. Losing weight
of body day by day, "I am
  a materialist," you said. Yet where did such

sublime sustaining chords *come* from?
Some shadowy *Am* that met desire?
  A secret potable source so simply there

you might just drink it up? Some strain
you could imagine playing on
  the violin you could no longer play?

3
Amused, you told how you had read
the words of praise, *holy holy*
  holy, had never meant, for the ancient Jews

who chanted them, that godhead had
some ineluctable goodness, superior
    moral presence; that *holy* only meant—

other, beyond, apart. So you
took our doings in the Land of Nod
    in stride. Our thrones and power, treasure, at last

were only holy . . . then the slackening,
a sovereignty of muscles lost,
    thews aflap on bones like weeds in a wind,

frame ever unexpectedly
slight when it began to prod
    skin, show through, bone charging on bone.

4

"What is the meaning of *prevail?*"
you asked one evening, who could not
    reach the button to raise your power chair.

You laughed and said it was *beyond* you,
a mountain in a dream. You found
    a sprig of holly for me; and I, this drop

of blood. Still the music—fresh,
potable, as you would think of it.
    I think of you that last October day,

wearing your helmet of cheer, a mask
above your pain; and most when once
    in autumn dusk the sun split open, orange

slices backing a skeletal tangle
of branches; glint of intellect scanning
    darkness like a flashlight, as if from one

of the pumpkins guarding your street like votives
leading to a presence; each eye a slash;
    sliced grin; a candle burning in each skull.

Station

All but missed his train, mesmerized by a mime on the platform. Under gray greasepaint, still as the Stone Statue he was to be taken for. Are you to tempt us, Vesuvian? Ashen survivor, hollow-eyed manikin out of Hades, harsh charmer waiting for offerings! His pasteboard coffer: *I am the Giver of Love and Joy* in blue Magic Marker scrawled on the lid.

"And the whole region of Pompeii inflamed the imagination of de Sade." Imploring, caring stare, body jerking to caress the air should chink of coin waken mummy limbs.

Solitude

Cretan farmers still press their olives. Swallow
retsina, tend their flocks. Our scholars know
—oracular computers tell them so—

it's just as the Minoans did. Do we
know them then, the Minoans? Is their debris
ours too? Rather consider to what degree

warehouse palaces are dazzlements,
and through the dark mullions of romance
see for once that we see nothing, nothing.

Serial

At one end altogether of whatever
length the strip could possibly be

you might follow the song of the warbler
like a thread paid out

like a line beautifully cast on a calm sea
specular in fiery noon

following in toward source, quarry,
judgment seat.

A line of birds has been drawn
over the horizon. Who could tell

where it had gone? The boy on the sailfish
was a dot on the past. You may not know

where it was he stood.
The length of a thread; the where you are.

Grand Hours

Because the red fox canters in dusk down the middle of the road, intent, smiling about something, grandmother's house perhaps, white tip of tail flowing out behind him, straight; because the fox is alone with him and he alone with the fox; because the fox has something white at the corner of his jaw, hanging, like a cigarette;

because the fox is gone then and he thinks, tail does not touch road, he holds it up to save grooming that plush bush; because he arrives out of the dark just as Gretel runs out of the mansion lifting a mammoth butterfly net;

because a bat is caught in the long bottom, grimy, tangling, dark bat panic from others taken in the hall; because the net has involved the bat, and it struggles—less and less; because Gretel imagines she has torn off a wing, and squeaks of panic come no longer;

because the net looks like stone-age coleslaw; because the bat is listening.

Because the bat spewed in Hans's mouth when it careened above the Scrabble and he must wash his mouth out—yet comes at last to help, "poor living thing," he croons; because the scissors loop by loop snip free until the bottom of the net lies on the night stones; because the light is snuffed, and rain comes.

Because the lane under beeches winds between borders of flowerets, meadow rue, trillium, butterflies wantoning, a pale doe silently across the lane looking, her shawled old-lady neck, ears cocked toward him; because her yearling toddles after, hindquarters like a little boy's in gray pants; because it is like a lamb and bends and nibbles, yes.

Because the deer in a grove of high grass, like touring intruders in a rose garden, peer as if through opera glasses at him.

Because they stand utterly still, then are gone: the Duke of Berry turns the leaf, moves his polished topaz over his *Hours* to magnify the creatures in borders of another leaf.

Shutters

"I walk this way most every day," he said;
"I've seen you working on your shutters." Redwings

were calling along the breeze, pine shadows rode
new grass. I turned to him; it was the neighbor.

He said, "if I'm disturbing you——." I showed
my palm and what might pass with him for stigma

from the screwdriver when I drove in the screws;
showed how I pinioned gudgeons to the jambs

and pintles to the shutters that the owner
of this house before me had removed, green panels,

louvers painted shut with coats unnumbered,
unnumbered years. "You're new in town; if you

don't have a church," he said, "why not"—and he
raised his boot to the stoop—"consider mine?"

He leaned there, bent on me. I went on kneeling,
studying my hand. The welt on the palm would redden,

darken to bruise. Already a stain was spreading
over life line and heart line. I heard the song

of Kohler's pond downhill: a redwing sang,
but not of our imaginings. He called

to his mate in rushes where the scum bloomed green;
mosquitoes hung there, too young to range beyond

the bullfrog's head agog. My neighbor took
advantage of the quiet. "You putting them up

to keep the sun out," he wanted to know, "or keep
what happens inside happening inside?" That

was no friendly thing to say, I thought and looked
at him as if I had not understood.

The scent of lilacs building into purple,
pausing to mix with whiffs of chalking paint,

hung at the porch side. He chuckled then, as if
to share a confidence. "My church," he said

standing to go, "is around the corner." When
the shutters were hung in their old places, I knew

the wind would blow them shut and open, back
and forth, for I had no shutter dogs. Come storms

they'd bang on clapboards, hard hands of my house
would clap and join the west wind charging around

the corners. I told him I caught his hint—hearing
my shutters clapping, echoing up the sky,

applause to all the region of my house.

Acknowledgments

For their encouragement, the author is indebted to the editors of the following publications for first publishing these poems, sometimes in different form:

Agni: "Stillness"
The Atlantic Monthly: "Worn Tool"
Green Mountains Review: "Home Reel," "Ohio in Italy"
Harvard Review: "Above Como" (as "Above Cadenabbia")
Hunger Mountain: "Shutters"
Mudfish: "Iris," "Hamster Hotel"
The New Yorker: "Instructions for Planting a Pine Woodlot"
Partisan Review: "Conclusion"
Pequod: "Natural History: A Barn"
Ploughshares: "Rain Date" (as "Rainy Sunday")
Poetry Porch: "Rain Crow"
The Saint Ann's Review: "Opera Orchard" (as "Opera Garden")
Salamander: "Ghazal for Geldzahler," "Sonam Lama"
Salmagundi: "Prepared Piano" (as "Altered Piano"), "Drier Air"
Seneca Review: "Grand Hours"
The Southern Review: "Bottleshard," "Halloween Away"
Southwest Review: "Stable" (as "Weather Permitting")
Tight: "Station"
The Yale Review: "On Looking into Lattimore's Homer"

"Serial" first appeared in *Words for Images: A Gallery of Poems*, edited by John Hollander and Joanna Weber (Yale University Art Gallery, 2001).

"Above Como" was delivered as the 2003 Phi Beta Kappa poem at Yale.

My thanks to the Rockefeller Foundation and Bellagio Study and Conference Center, where some of these poems were written. Thanks also to the Corporation of Yaddo for hospitality during valuable residencies.

"Cardinals" is for my mother, an expert whistler, who conversed with her favorite birds.

"Conclusion" alludes to Brueghel's painting *Landscape with the Fall of Icarus.*

"Ghazal for Geldzahler": Henry Geldzahler (1935–1994) was an art critic, curator of twentieth-century painting at the Metropolitan Museum of Art, New York City Commissioner for Cultural Affairs, and starred in a Warhol film.

"Halloween Away" is for John Swan. Lake Itasca is the source of the Mississippi River.

"Ohio in Italy" is for James Wright.

"Prepared Piano" is for David Porter. John Cage composed several pieces for piano in which the strings were to be clamped, pinned, etc.

"Safe Mode": Rovers on Mars are in safe mode when shut down and awaiting instructions.

"Serial" was written as a response to Mark Rothko's *Untitled*, 1954 (Yale University Art Gallery).